BUT WHAT DID GOD SAY?

Sophia Strown

© 2019 Divine Works Publishing

BUT WHAT DID GOD SAY?

ALL RIGHTS RESERVED. No part of this publication may be reproduced, stored in a retrieval system, or transmitted in any form or by any means, electronic, mechanical, photocopying, recording or otherwise without the prior permission of the publisher or in accordance with the provisions of the Copyright, Designs, and Patents Act 1988 or under the terms of any license permitting limited copying issued by the Copyright Licensing Agency.

Scripture taken from the New King James Version®. Copyright © 1982 by Thomas Nelson. Used by permission. All rights reserved.

Scripture quotations marked (NIV) are taken from the Holy Bible, New International Version®, NIV®. Copyright © 1973, 1978, 1984, 2011 by Biblica, Inc.™ Used by permission of Zondervan. All rights reserved worldwide. www.zondervan.com The "NIV" and "New International Version" are trademarks registered in the United States Patent and Trademark Office by Biblica, Inc.™

Scripture taken from the New Century Version®. Copyright © 2005 by Thomas Nelson. Used by permission. All rights reserved.

Scripture quotations marked (MSG) are taken from THE MESSAGE. Copyright © by Eugene H. Peterson 1993, 2002, 2018. Used by permission of NavPress. All rights reserved. Represented by Tyndale House Publishers, a Division of Tyndale House Ministries.

ISBN: 978-1-949105-19-3 (paperback)
ISBN: 978-1-949105-20-9 (eBook)

Published by:
Divine Works Publishing, LLC
Royal Palm Beach, Florida USA

www.DivineWorksPublishing.com
561-990-BOOK (2665)

Table of Contents

Part I: I Hear You God!
Perfect Plans 3
Come as You Are 7
Kingdom Over Culture 11
What About Your Friends? 15
Healthy and Whole 19

Part II: I'm So Excited For What I've Heard!
I Can and I Will 25
A Prepared Place 29
Focus on Yourself 33
No Fear 37
Victory is Mine 41

Part III: This is Not as Easy as I thought it Would Be!
Chosen 45
Worth the Wait 51
Be Still 55
The Real Enemy 59
No More Worries 63

Part IV: Wait, Did I Actually Hear "You" God?
Enemy's Plans Exposed 69
What Are You Thinking? 73
At the Right Time 77
You Are Going to Make it 81
Labor Pains 85

Part V: I'm Choosing to Believe Anyway!
What is Peace? 89
All Things 95
Can You Imagine? 99
It is So 103
Try Again 107

Part VI: I'm Actually Seeing it Coming Forth!
Believe it Before You See it 111
God, You Promised 117
Brand New 121
Keeping Promises 125
Any Day Now 129

Prayer For Spiritual Wisdom

Part I:
I Hear You God!

Perfect Plans

*For I know the plans that I have for you,
"declares the Lord," plans to prosper you and not to harm
you, plans to give you hope and a future.
(Jeremiah 29:11, NIV)*

God's will and plan for your life is perfect. He has written a pretty amazing story for your life. He knows everything about you, what makes you happy, what makes you sad, even the amount of hairs on your head. God had a grand blueprint in mind when He created you. His plans are never to hurt or harm you. God's plan is always to protect, strengthen, and mold you into the person he saw before you were formed in your mother's womb. Embrace whatever it is he is doing in your current season. God doesn't waste any experience, everything will ultimately piece together to complete the perfect puzzle that He designed.

Prayer

Heavenly Father,

Your plans for me are always good and perfect.

What an honor and privilege it is

that I call you Father.

I can trust that with you,

even on my darkest days,

that my future is bright!

In Jesus Name, Amen

Notes

Come As You Are

Jesus answered and said to them, " Those who are well have no need of a physician, but those who are sick. I have come not to call the righteous, but sinners, to repentance."
(Luke 5:31-32, NKJV)

One of the biggest lies that the enemy will try to convince you is that you have to get yourself all the way together and cleaned up before you go before Jesus. This inaccuracy has caused many to think that they are not worthy of being in the presence of Jesus, and this had led to many not receiving the deliverance that they so badly need. Believers are no longer subjected to the religious laws of man, but instead we receive new grace and mercy every day. Bring every part of you to the altar; this is the only place where your life will alter. Jehovah Rapha is waiting to restore you.

Prayer

Heavenly Father,

You are a God of conviction and not condemnation.

I can come to you just as I am,

but I will not leave the same way.

Jesus came and purchased my freedom

that I would be able confess my sins and be made new.

Thank you for the gift of salvation

through Jesus Christ.

In Jesus Name, Amen

Notes

Kingdom Over Culture

And do not be conformed to this world, but be transformed by the renewing of your mind, that you may prove what is that good and acceptable and perfect will of God.
(Romans 12:2, NKJV)

You are called to be in this world, but not of this world. In other words, you are a part of the kingdom and not a part of the culture. You know the saying, " Do it for the culture?" It should actually be " Do it for the kingdom. " As sons and daughters of the Most High God, you have an obligation to be the hands and feet of Jesus in all things that you do. You are a representation of Christ on earth. So you have a duty to display His love in everything. You want to fit in, but you were created to stand out. You must understand that you will not be accepted into something that you were sent to influence, which means you will have to be set apart in order to fulfill your responsibilities as a follower of Jesus. People will notice the difference in you, and that's OK. That is God's plan; they will see Him in you and want to know more. You are called to be a living example of what is good, acceptable, and the perfect will of your father in heaven.

Prayer

Heavenly Father,

Thank You for a renewed and transformed mind.

I have been called to serve You and display Your goodness

and glory everywhere that I go.

I do not take this responsibility lightly.

I will not conform to the culture;

instead I will influence the culture to

conform to Your kingdom.

In Jesus Name, Amen

Notes

What About Your Friends?

One who has unreliable friends soon comes to ruins, but there is a friend that sticks closer than a brother.
(Proverbs 18:24, NIV)

Where God is taking you, there are just simply some people that cannot go. If you hold on to relationships that God is asking you to release, you can delay and/or forfeit your promise altogether. God gave that promise to a certain version of you, and you cannot become that version if you are intertwined with expired connections. God has divine connections and Kingdom relationships waiting to help you accomplish His agenda. Release who God is asking you to release so that you can receive what He is trying to give.

Prayer

Heavenly Father,

Search every relationship, partnership, and friendship in my life. Remove every connection that was not sent by you. Whether the connection is expired or ungodly, detach me from any person, place or thing that would delay me from fulfilling my call in Your kingdom. I ask for wisdom and understanding to trust that whoever and whatever I have to set free is for my good.

In Jesus Name, Amen

Notes

Healthy and Whole

*He sent His word and healed them,
and delivered them from their destruction.
(Psalms 107:20, NKJV)*

Healing is your portion! God's word says that by Jesus' stripes we are healed and made whole. As declared in Matthew 18:18, whatever you bind on earth shall be bound in heaven, and whatever you loose on earth shall be loosed in heaven. So bind up sickness, and loose the healing powers of Jesus. This is your inheritance as sons and daughters of the Most High God. It is already settled in heaven, and it will be done on earth for you.

Prayer

Heavenly Father,

Anyone that has faith and stands on Your Word will see a manifestation of supernatural healings. Send the comforter, Your Holy Spirit to the reader in this moment. Let Holy Spirit sweep their hearts, minds, bodies, and even their homes. Remove all plagues of the wicked one. The stripes and the lashes that Jesus bore make them well. I decree and declare that sickness, suicidal thoughts, anxiety, fear, and depression have to bow to the power and authority of Jesus. These things are no match for the power of our Almighty God. Thank You that health and wholeness is our portion.

In Jesus Name, Amen

Notes

Part II:
I'm So Excited For What I've Heard!

I Can and I Will

I can do all things through Christ who strengthens me.
(Philippians 4:13, NKJV)

There's nothing too hard for the Lord, absolutely nothing! When you view difficult situations through your own human capabilities, it becomes very easy to get discouraged, and allow fear and doubt to creep in. Jesus promises that if you lean on Him and trust Him, you can do all things. In your own strength times of hardship can be next to impossible to overcome, but with the power and authority that you receive through Christ Jesus, you can and you will overcome any challenge.

Prayer

Heavenly Father,

There is nothing too big or too small for you.

You're almighty, omnipotent, and omnipresent.

Saturate me with Your peace and power, strengthen me,

and teach me how to rely on You and only You

because this is how the impossible becomes possible.

In Jesus Name, Amen

Notes

A Prepared Place

A man's gift makes room for him,
and brings him before great men.
(Proverbs 18:16, NKJV)

There may be other singers, dancers, artists, teachers, doctors, lawyers, ministers, or whatever the thing is that you're gifted at. God tailor made your gifts and talents just for you. God has created a sphere of influence that only you and your gifts can flourish in. There are people that only you can reach, so there is no need to compete or compare yourself to others with similar gifting's. God has given you a grace and an anointing to thrive in a space that He has set aside for you. God is developing you in the dark room, but when the time is right, He will move you from the shadows to the sunlight.

Prayer

Heavenly Father,

You've anointed and crowned me with Your favor,

and Your favor has gone before me and created an

environment for me to excel in my gifts.

I have favor with God and man, and this will grant me

opportunities that I could've only dreamed of.

I never ever have to battle, wrestle, or contend for a spot

because You've given me a lane of my own.

Thank You.

In Jesus Name, Amen

Notes

Focus on Yourself

Stay Calm; mind your own business; do your own job. You've heard all this from us before, but a reminder never hurts.
(I Thessalonians 4:11, MSG)

Worry about yourself! You have to be the CEO of minding the business that pays you. We have 20/20 vision when it comes to the mistakes of others, but that is not your concern. Your focus should not be on them, but you should be focused on what God is asking of you. One distraction can cost you dearly. We've all had a coworker that couldn't do their job properly because they were too concerned with how you were doing yours. Don't be that coworker. As believers, we are all coworkers in the kingdom laboring together to accomplish the plans of God. Mind your business and do the job you were appointed to do. God will separate the wheat from the tares.

Prayer

Heavenly Father,

Keep me calm, minding my business,

and focused on the job assigned to me.

Eliminate distractions that would tempt me

to worry about the work of others.

Elevate me above the noise

so that I may continue to work diligently unto You.

In Jesus Name, Amen

Notes

No Fear

For God has not given us a spirit of fear,
but of power, love, and a sound mind.
(II Timothy 1:7, NKJV)

Naturally, when you encounter unknown things or situations, one would be tempted to be afraid. To quote Bob Proctor, " Faith and fear both demand that you believe in something that you cannot see." So why not choose the belief that something good will happen. God is not the author of fear; His word says that He is the author and finisher of our faith. (Hebrews 12:2) God has given us power, love, and a sound mind, and most importantly, He has given us His word, which is good and true. Choose to rebuke fear and embrace faith.

Prayer

Heavenly Father,

As I encounter unknown situations,

help me to remember that I do not have to be afraid

because You are with me every step of the way.

The will of God will never take me where Your grace will not

sustain me, or where Your covering will not protect me.

I choose to believe that something good will happen.

Thank You for a sound mind.

In Jesus Name, Amen

Notes

Victory is Mine

No weapon formed against you shall prosper.
(Isaiah 54:17, NKJV)

Everyone has a purpose for the kingdom of God, and the enemy will wage war against that purpose, especially those of you that have a high call in the Kingdom. The word says that the enemy walks around like a roaring lion seeking whom he can devour. I say this not to incite fear, but to make you aware of the enemy's mission. God never said the weapons wouldn't form, He said they would not prosper. So when the enemy comes to attack, don't shrink back into a victim mindset, instead rise up as the victor that you are in Christ Jesus. Spoiler Alert: the fight is fixed; Jesus already won the victory for you at the cross! Open your mouth and declare your victory!

Prayer

Heavenly Father,

Thank You for the hedge of protection that you've placed

around these your sons and daughters.

Thank you that your light and love surrounds and protects

them like a shield, and nothing can penetrate that shield

that is not of you.

Your Holy Spirit goes out before them and clears the way,

knocking back all things seen and unseen that are not of You.

They are covered under the blood of the lamb,

and no evil can befall them.

In Jesus Name, Amen

Notes

Part III:
This is Not as Easy as I thought it Would Be!

Chosen

For many are called, but few are chosen.
(Matthew 22:14, NKJV)

In Acts 1, the people were told to wait for the promised Holy Spirit to show up. There were many people told to wait, but the majority decided not to wait. When the promise actually showed up, there were only a few people there. These people are often referred to as the remnant. See many were asked to wait around, but only a few chose to stand and wait on the promise of God. Like the parable Jesus spoke about in Matthew 22 many are called into the kingdom to do the work and will of our Father, but few choose to make the necessary sacrifices and do the work. Make a decision today that you will be a remnant person, when everyone else walks away because things are hard and the wait is long, you will choose to stand firm and wait on the promises of the Father. You were chosen for such a time as this!

Prayer

Heavenly Father,

I was not just called, but I am one of the chosen few,

and I am so grateful that you saw fit to choose me.

I understand the weight and responsibility that comes with

being chosen, and I will not abandon my position.

I will stand firm on Your word and accomplish Your will.

All the glory and honor belongs to You.

In Jesus Name, Amen

Notes

Worth the Wait

*But those who wait on the LORD shall renew their strength;
They shall mount up with wings like eagles, They shall run
and not be weary, They shall walk and not faint.
(Isaiah 40:31, NKJV)*

Wait; to stay where one is or delay action until a particular time or something else happens. Waiting is one of the most difficult things most of us will ever be asked to do because it's hard for us to wait when we feel like we deserve it now. We tend to desire instant gratification and we want the harvest as soon as you plant the seeds. You expect the promise as soon as you step out on faith, but this is just not how God works. In an attempt to fulfill the need to have things now, you often get ahead of God's timing. This is dangerous because it can lead you down a path of frustration, exhaustion, doubt, and sometimes make you give up all together. God did not give you that word to make you anxious, but so that you could rest and have peace while you wait. That word is a mighty weapon. Wait upon the Lord, He will prove himself!

Prayer

Heavenly Father,

Your word says that You know my end from the beginning. You know every roadblock, every detour, and every attack of the enemy that would tempt me to not wait on You.

Remind me that no matter what I may be facing today, You have already gone before me and You have complete control. I will choose to wait upon You. Thank You for a refreshing of your spirit and the building up of my spirit man so that I can endure that wait and possess the promise.

In Jesus Name, Amen

Notes

Be Still

Be still, and know that I am God; I will be exalted among the nations, I will be exalted in the earth.
(Psalms 46:10, NKJV)

Each day you are ripping and running, calendar packed, and you barely have a moment to spare. I know you probably think you have to physically move about to accomplish the plan of God for your life, and this is partially true, but there are moments when God will ask you to be still. The purpose of being still is so that he may be exalted. He needs you to know that what he has done/will do couldn't have been accomplished in your merit. When you get still, the noise of everyday life is silenced, and you can hear His still small voice clearly. God can do more in your one moment of stillness than you could ever do in a lifetime of physical work. The end result will be a supernatural victory/breakthrough in your life, and God will be exalted and He will receive all the glory.

Prayer

Heavenly Father,

The enemy wants me to believe that busyness is a requirement. This is a subtle tactic to distract me from hearing and being able to obey your commands.

There may come a time when I will be asked to be still,

and I will choose to be still

and allow you to be exalted in my life.

In Jesus Name, Amen

Notes

The Real Enemy

For we do not wrestle against flesh and blood, but against principalities, against powers, against the rulers of the darkness of this age, against spiritual hosts of wickedness in the heavenly places. (Ephesians 6:12, NKJV)

There is a real war going on for your soul and your destiny, and if you are not careful to identify the actual source of the warfare, you will launch an attack on the wrong target. You are not at war with your family, your friends, your coworkers, your boss, that barista at Starbucks, or the driver that cut you off. Those are only vessels that spirits have chosen to manifest themselves in. When we realize who the real enemy is, we will no longer be ignorant to the schemes of the adversary. Knowledge of whom and what you are warring against will better equip you to defend yourself against the attacks. Your weapon, God's word, will lead you into victory.

Prayer

Heavenly Father,

Because I am not wrestling against flesh and blood, I need a heightened level of discernment that can only be accomplished through spending time with you.

Help me to have the wisdom and understanding to recognize the most finely crafted tactic of the enemy.

Thank You that I am able to enter into this wrestling match with the armor of God and conquer the enemy.

In Jesus Name, Amen

Notes

No More Worries

For after all these things the gentiles seek. For your heavenly Father knows that you need all these things. But seek first the kingdom of God and His righteousness, and all these things shall be added to you. Therefore do not worry about tomorrow, for tomorrow will worry about its own things. Sufficient for the day is its own trouble.
(Matthew 6:32-34, NKJV)

You cannot worry and worship at the same time, as one contradicts the other. You must make the choice to trust God. Matthew 6 explains how God cares for the birds and the flowers. He knows when they need rain, sunshine, shelter, and food. The animals and the plants don't have to wonder if they'll get what they need, it's God's design that they receive every need right when they are supposed to. You are worth much more to God, so why wouldn't He do the same for you? He can and He will. No matter the circumstances that you may face, God said that if you seek Him first all of His righteousness will be added unto you. So, seek Him!

Prayer

Heavenly Father,

I choose to cancel my subscription to worry magazine and

devote myself daily to worshipping you.

Through all circumstances, I will trust you.

Every need that I have,

no matter how big or small will be met,

according to your word.

In Jesus Name, Amen

Notes

Part IV:
Wait, Did I Actually Hear "You" God?

Enemy's Plans Exposed

*The thief comes to steal, kill, and destroy.
I have come so that you may have life
and have it more abundantly.
(John 10:10, NKJV)*

To steal, kill, and destroy, this is not one big assignment of the enemy, but these are three separate attacks. We've all heard people or maybe we've declared victory over the enemy, saying, "I made it through", but their joy, hope, faith, or optimism didn't. They are not even aware that the assignment wasn't to kill or destroy, but to steal. So the enemy's attempt was actually a success. You cannot be ignorant to the enemy's schemes and devices. You must be able to discern the weapon so that you can conquer, defeat, and destroy the enemy. Through Jesus you receive a promise of an abundant life, but you cannot collect on that promise if you allow the thief to come in and steal what rightfully belongs to you.

Prayer

Heavenly Father,

May the eyes of my understanding be enlightened

that I would not be blinded

to the plots and plans of the enemy.

Through Jesus, the life of abundance is already mine.

May everything that the enemy has stolen

be returned sevenfold.

In Jesus Name, Amen

Notes

What Are You Thinking?

Casting down arguments and every high thing that exalts itself against the knowledge of God, bringing every thought into captivity to the obedience of Christ
(II Corinthians 10:5, NKJV)

Thoughts become words, words become beliefs, and beliefs then become actions. Everything starts with a thought. If the enemy can gain control over your thought life, he can hold you captive with his lies. This is why it is imperative to know the word of God. When the enemy comes in with his lies and accusations, God's word empowers you with the knowledge to fight back and cast down the lies and command that they come into obedience with Christ. As a believer and follower of Christ, you have the power and authority to make a demand on heaven. Your thoughts and circumstances then have no choice, but to fall in line and meet your demands. It may not happen immediately, but keep taking things captive; eventually things have to conform to the word of God.

Prayer

Heavenly Father,

Thank You for Jesus! Your word says that Jesus came to set the captives free. Many of us are being held captive to the lies of the enemy, but his time has run out!

Let Your truth emerge in these Your sons and daughters.

I plead the blood of Jesus over their minds. When Jesus was raised up, so were they, free and victorious.

Let every single plot, ploy, plan, scheme, and devise of the enemy to control their thoughts be canceled now in Jesus name.

Every single lie that the enemy has tried to make them believe will be taken captive and made to obey the words of Christ!

In Jesus Name, Amen

Notes

At the Right Time

For the vision is yet for an appointed time; but at the end it will speak, and will not lie. Though it tarries, wait for it; because surely it will come, it will not tarry.
(Habakkuk 2:3, NKJV)

In 2 Peter, God declares that he is not slow in keeping his promises, as we understand slowness. God is not in a rush, you are! The vision has a scheduled date to manifest, and you will most likely not be told when that will be. Do not grow impatient and think that the vision is tarrying (lingering or taking a long time). God clearly said, it will happen at the appointed time and will not tarry. It will manifest in God's time, not yours. Surrender your timeline for God's perfect timing, and watch how things begin to shift.

Prayer

Heavenly Father,

Thank You that although it seems like I've been waiting

a long time for the vision to come to pass,

it is actually right on schedule.

Father sometimes I feel like the waiting process

from the vision to the manifestation

seems like punishment.

Please remind me that it is only preparation.

You love me too much to give me something

that I am not prepared to receive.

You will do exactly as You've promised in Your time.

In Jesus Name, Amen

Notes

You Are Going to Make it

But He said to them, " Why are you fearful, O you of little faith?" Then He arose and rebuked the winds and the sea, and there was a great calm.
(Matthew 8:26, NKJV)

Jesus and the disciples get into the boat with the intention of going to the other side. A strong storm arises while Jesus is sleeping, and the disciples start to panic, assuming they will perish. They awaken Jesus. He rebukes the winds and calms the waves. When Jesus stepped in that boat, there was no other option other than for the boat to reach the other side because that was the word that Jesus spoke when He got inside the boat. That boat is your life, the storm of life begins to rage, but Jesus is with you. You don't have to panic or be afraid; you will arrive at your intended destination because that is the word that was spoken for you. Fear not and rest knowing that when you accepted Jesus as your savior, he stepped in your boat, and you will always be safe in the hands of the Almighty God.

Prayer

Heavenly Father,

When the storms of life come flooding in

and I feel like I am about to drown,

remind me that Jesus is always with me and that I can rest.

Jesus will speak a word and the storm must obey.

I will make it to my destiny.

I have no other option because You've declared so.

In Jesus Name, Amen

Notes

Labor Pains

"In the same way I will not cause pain without allowing something new to be born," says the Lord. "If I cause you pain, I will not stop you from giving birth to your new nation, " says your God.
(Isaiah 66:9, NCV)

Labor pains are a part of the birthing process; there is just no way to avoid the pain during birth. In a natural childbirth there is an option to receive an epidural, this makes the pain more tolerable. In the supernatural, God has given you a comforter as well, His Holy Spirit, to sustain you during the supernatural birthing process. God will never allow you to go through hurtful and difficult situations without it birthing something new in you. You may be hurting, you may be in pain, you may be tired, and you may be broken, but keep pushing. There is purpose in your pain.

Prayer

Heavenly Father,

Thank You for the ultimate comforter, Your Holy Spirit.

I never have to endure the pain of life alone.

The Holy Spirit is always with me, ready and willing

to alleviate some of the pain.

Thank You for increasing my tolerance so that I can

keep pushing to the promise.

In Jesus Name, Amen

Notes

Part V:
I'm Choosing to Believe Anyway!

What is Peace?

You will keep him in perfect peace,
whose mind is stayed on You,
because he trusts in You.
(Isaiah 26:3, NKJV)

Peace can be defined as being untroubled, tranquil, or content. The definition of perfect is to bring to completion; finish; to make flawless or faultless; complete or beyond practical. So in other words, God is saying that He will keep you in a complete, flawless, faultless state of tranquility, contentment, and stillness that is beyond practical behavior. But, there's one condition, you MUST keep your mind focused on Him. I know there are many things competing for your attention, and it's easy to get distracted and lose sight of what's most important, and that is that you must keep God at the center of our focus at all times. This is the only way that you can receive and keep His perfect peace.

Prayer

Heavenly Father,

Your word promises to keep me in perfect peace, but only if I keep my mind stayed on you. I must admit that my mind has not been set on you. I've allowed the trials and tribulations of the world to become my focal point. Because you are not seated in your rightful place in my heart and mind, I've experienced much turmoil and anxiety. Father today I make the choice to silence that noise that is in competition with you. I surrender completely, I receive the gift of peace, and I place every concern and worry where they belong, at the feet of Jesus. I will not worry about the job, the house, the finances, or the medical diagnosis. I don't have to sit and wonder how everything will work out. My job is to trust You, and Your job is to come through and do as you've said. I will focus on You and only You because I trust You.

In Jesus Name, Amen

Notes

All Things

*And we know that all things work together
for the good of those who love God,
to those who are called according
to His purpose.
(Romans 8:28, NKJV)*

Not Just some things or most things, but all things will work together for your good. Every single setback, every heartbreak, every disappointment, and ever unfair circumstance are pages in your book of life. The good, the bad, and the ugly all are essential to fulfill God's intent for you. Rest knowing that every single aspect of your life has been carefully planned, and in the end EVERYTHING will be proven to be for your benefit.

Prayer

Heavenly Father,

Thank You for being my mountain mover,

my promise keeper, my miracle worker,

and my light when it's dark.

I choose to take You at Your word and

trust that You are working all things out for my good,

even when I can't see it, I will trust You.

In Jesus Name, Amen

Notes

Can You Imagine?

But it is written: " Eye, has not seen, nor ear heard, nor have entered into the heart of man the things which God has prepared for those who love Him."
(I Corinthians 2:9, NKJV)

God's plan for you has never been seen or heard of in the way that He will do it for you. He is the ultimate chef, and He has prepared a specialty order just for you. Whatever your wildest dream or imagination is, God is going above and beyond what you can envision. Above and beyond all that you could ever ask or imagine. (Ephesians 3:20) He is omnipotent! Your human brain cannot even fathom the goodness He has in store for you. Prepare to have your mind BLOWN!

Prayer

Heavenly Father,

You are the almighty God

and nothing is impossible for you.

I wait with eager expectation for you to show up

and do what eyes haven't seen and ears haven't heard

as declared in Your word.

In Jesus Name, Amen

Notes

It is So

So shall My word be that goes forth from My mouth;
it shall not return to Me void,
but it shall accomplish that which I please,
and it shall prosper in the thing for which I sent it.
(Isaiah 55:11, NKJV)

God has a word for your life, even through hard times; we must continue to stand in faith. The enemy comes to kill, steal and destroy, but Jesus came that you may have life, and have it more abundantly (John 10:10). Now, make no mistakes, the enemy will attack, emotions will rise, and reality will not always look like the word that God spoke for your life. It's in these intense moments that we are tempted to quit, but we mustn't grow weary, we must seek the will of God even harder. Stand your ground and ask yourself " but what did God say?" His word is true, His word is eternal, and His word will NOT return to him void. It will accomplish the very thing that it was sent to do!

Prayer

Heavenly Father,

You are almighty! You speak a word over my life and it cannot and will not return to you until it has accomplished the task for which it was sent. I can rest knowing that regardless what I may be facing today, as long as I am in alignment with You and committed to Your will and purpose for my life, the seed (Your word) that You planted in me will produce fruit and what a mighty harvest it will be!

In Jesus Name, Amen

Notes

Try Again

And He said to them, "Cast your net on the right side of the and you will find some." So they cast, and now they were not able to draw it in because of the multitude of fish.
(John 21:6, NKJV)

Cast your nets again! The disciples had been fishing all night and caught nothing. Jesus shows up the next morning and instructs them to cast their nets out into the sea again. They obliged, and they caught so many fish that they couldn't take it all in. Maybe you started a business, went back to school, or stepped out to pursue a dream that didn't work out. Well, morning has come and Jesus is here. Cast your nets again, but this time with Jesus and watch the multitudes pour in.

Prayer

Heavenly Father,

Nothing You put Your hands on can fail,

not me, not my dreams, absolutely nothing!

Maybe the times that I tried before

were not God's appointed time,

but now Jesus has shown up and given me the green light.

You have crowned me with Your favor and goodness.

I will cast my nets again, and draw in

the multitudes of blessings you have given to me.

In Jesus Name, Amen

Notes

Part VI:
I'm Actually Seeing it Coming Forth!

Believe it Before You See It

Jesus said to her,
"Did I not say to you that if you would
believe you would see the glory of God?"
(John 11:40, NKJV)

You don't have to see how the plan will unfold or try to figure out how it will work. Faith works best when you believe before you see. You must believe that God can and will do as He's promised. It's God's job to show up and fulfill His promise. Lazarus, whom Jesus loved, was sick, his sisters sent word to ask Jesus to come and heal him. Jesus waited two days before he started to journey towards Lazarus and by the time He arrived, Lazarus had been dead for 4 days. When Jesus finally arrives Martha greets Him. Martha is pretty upset, but she still knows that God will do whatever Jesus asks of Him. Jesus calls Lazarus out of the grave and he comes forth. Lazarus can be viewed as your promise, you've believed, fasted, and prayed for, but it hasn't happened yet, possibly even looks dead. Jesus arrives and calls that thing to spring back to life. Sometimes we are praying to God for a healing miracle (quick fix), but God allows that thing to completely die so that He can perform a resurrection. You have to continue to believe like Martha, even when it's dead,

God can speak one word and resuscitate it, and everyone will see the glory of God.

Prayer

Heavenly Father,

You make all things new and cause dead things to rise.

Thank you for breathing new life into my dreams and me. I will continue to believe before I see. I wanted a quick fix, but You needed more time and because I had to wait, I received more than what was expected. I was praying for a healing, but You planned a resurrection. Thank You!

In Jesus Name, Amen

Notes

God, You Promised

*This charge I commit to you, son Timothy,
according to the prophecies previously
made concerning you, that by them you
may wage good warfare.
(I Timothy 1:18, NKJV)*

Prophecies can be summed up as God ordained words spoken before the event occurs. Paul was reminding his spiritual son Timothy that these words are weapons of warfare. On the road to purpose, the enemy will attack in an attempt to distract, detour, or destroy you from reaching the destiny God has for you. Remember the previous prophecies and declare them with boldness. No matter what the current situation is, God will not fail you. Write down every prophecy you receive, you will need them on your journey. When the road gets tough, pull out that list and declare them out of your mouth. God is a watcher over His word, and when you speak them out of your mouth, He has no choice but to move. God's promises are yes and amen, and you will see every single promise that was made to you. Stay strong, keep fighting, you are more than able through Christ to Triumph.

Prayer

Heavenly Father,

I can count on You! You will do exactly what You've said. I will not let what I see with my natural eyes distort what You've shown me in the spirit. I trust You, and I will wage war and fight the good fight with every word that You've ever given me. I am a mighty warrior and more than a conqueror because I belong to You. I will not give up and I will not give in, I must see every promise come to pass. Thank You for never giving up on me.

In Jesus Name, Amen

Notes

Brand New

Do not remember the former things,
Nor consider the things of the old.
Behold, I will do a new thing,
Now shall it spring forth; Shall you not know it?
I will even make a road in the wilderness
and rivers in the desert.
(Isaiah 43:18-19, NKJV)

Let go of the old and embrace the new! God wants you to not recall the former things or even consider the old things. God is trying to do something brand new for you. He will take the most inopportune situation and turn it into the biggest blessing you've ever seen. Release all of your old habits, the old job, the old relationships, and the old mindset and watch God show up with unexpected, uncommon, and unusual favor that will make a way where there seemed to be no way. Just watch, He is going to blow your mind!

Prayer

Heavenly Father,

I must admit that there are days when I want that old thing back. The old thing was comfortable, safe, and predictable. Pursuing the new thing is scary at times. Reality starts to clash with Your declarations, and I want to go running back to my place of comfort. Impart into me a supernatural portion of resilience so that I can deny the urge to go back to the former things, and embrace the new thing you are trying to do!

In Jesus Name, Amen

Notes

Keeping Promises

God is not a man, that He should lie,
Nor a son of man, that He should repent.
Has He said, and will He not do?
Or has He spoken, and will He not make it good?
(Numbers 23:19, NKJV)

God is not going to play you! You can't always count on those around you to keep their word and do as they promised, and you tend to view God in the way we view those around us. Therefore, you don't feel like you can't relinquish all of your trust to him. You can't treat God like he is man. You can whole-heartedly trust that if He said it; He will do exactly what he said! God is not like man; He cannot and will not lie! Your current circumstances may not appear to be in line with God's word, but at the appointed time, He will show up and make good on his word. Stay in faith and keep trusting Him!

Prayer

Heavenly Father,

Thank You that your word is true!

Unlike the word of man,

I can stand firm trusting you.

No matter the situation or circumstance,

I know that you will do exactly what you said!

In Jesus Name, Amen

Notes

Any Day Now

"Yes indeed, it will not be long now". God's Decree. Things are going to happen so fast that your head will swim, one thing fast on the heels of the other. You won't be able to keep up. Everything will be happening all at once- and everywhere you look, blessings! (Amos 9:13, MSG)

You are closer than you think! Any day now, the floodgates of heaven will open and shower you with God's promises. You've fasted, you've prayed, you've kept an expectant heart, and most of all you've remained obedient. The process gets a little difficult here and you become tempted to quit because you don't know that you are close to a breakthrough. Let me explain using the example of childbirth. Labor and delivery is a very painful experience for most and usually very intense. The woman is pushing and pushing for some, hours and hours go by. There's a strong urge to want to give up and say " I can't do this anymore", but right at that moment, the doctor says, " I can see the head, a couple more pushes and we're done". You see, the woman doesn't know how extremely close she is to birthing her promise (the baby) and the process becomes almost unbearable, but right as she's about to give up, the promise shows up and the pain and frustration is no comparison to the joy she feels. Liken your situation to giving birth and you're in labor. It won't be long; soon you'll be holding the promise and the blessings of God will overtake you. Hang in there and don't you dare give up! There's a promise on the other side of your pain.

Prayer

Heavenly Father,

Thank You for the strength to endure the labor pains. It is through this process that You show me how strong I really am. Thank You for being my birthing coach and helping me continue to push when I become tempted to give up. Any day now, I will see the fulfillment of Your promise, and everywhere that I turn there will be blessings.

All of the glory and honor belongs to you!

In Jesus Name, Amen

Notes

PRAYER FOR SPIRITUAL WISDOM
Ephesians 1:17-23, NKJV (paraphrase)

I pray that the God of our Lord Jesus Christ, the Father of glory, may give to me the spirit of wisdom and revelation in the knowledge of Him, the eyes of my understanding being enlightened; that I may know what is the hope of His calling, what are the riches of the glory of His inheritance in the saints, and what is the exceeding greatness of His power toward us who believe, according to the working of His mighty power which He worked in Christ when He raised Him from the dead and seated Him at His right hand in the heavenly places, far above all principality and power and might and dominion, and every name that is named, not only in this age but also in which is to come. And He put all things under His feet, and gave Him to be head over all things to the church, which is His body, the fullness of Him who feels all in all. In Jesus Name, Amen

Notes

About the Author

Sophia Strown is a certified Life Coach with a heart and passion to help others who are trying to reach their purpose in life. She is originally from Pell City, AL yet spent an extensive amount of her former years in Memphis, TN and currently resides in the Tampa Bay, FL area. Sophia offers encouragement to those who may have lost their way in this tumultuous journey we call life. She provides inspiring and motivating guidance from both a Biblical standpoint as well as personal life experience. Understanding that we all make mistakes and fall short, Sophia's insight comes with the conviction and love of Christ that propels you to strive for a better day.

www.ingramcontent.com/pod-product-compliance
Lightning Source LLC
Chambersburg PA
CBHW072022110526
44592CB00012B/1399